The Savvy Traveler's Guide To Fun Down Under

MELBOURNE, SYDNEY, AND CAIRNS,
AUSTRALIA
AUCKLAND, NEW ZEALAND
AND BEACHCOMBER ISLAND, FIJI

Caitlyn E. Moore

Renton, Washington

All rights reserved. No part of this book may be used or reproduced by any means, graphic, electronic, or mechanical, including photocopying, recording, taping or by any information storage retrieval system without the written permission of the publisher except in the case of brief quotations embodied in critical articles and reviews.

Moonlight Garden Publications
an imprint of Gazebo Gardens Publishing
www.GazeboGardensPublishing.com

Edited by S. C. Moore
Photography by Caitlyn E. Moore (except where noted)

Copyright 2013.

All rights reserved.
Printed in the United States of America.

ISBN: 978-1-938281-00-6 (paperback)
ISBN: 978-1-938281-01-3   (e-book)

Library of Congress Control Number: 2013945544

To my parents, who have encouraged me
and given me the incredible opportunity
to fulfill my dreams and desires
to travel and study abroad.

INTRODUCTION

When I was a little girl, I imagined traveling to faraway lands but never thought those dreams would come true. Yet, as a young adult, I have explored castles, hiked through ruins, paddled on the ocean, and trudged through the jungle. Influenced by my dreams to travel and my experiences abroad, I developed an appreciation for foreign cultures and a desire to write about them, which inspired me to create the *Savvy Traveler's* books series.

The first exotic world I had the pleasure of visiting was Hawaii, during family vacations. From the time I was an infant, I grew up learning about the culture and enjoying the beauty of the islands. This instilled in me a yearning to discover new and different places.

At age eleven, my parents took me to England, Wales, and Ireland. I was full of excitement, wonder, and a thirst for knowledge, and I began journaling about my experiences.

I ventured to Peru and Bolivia with my parents when I was fourteen. During my explorations of Lima, Machu Picchu, Lake Titicaca, and the Amazon Jungle, and my interactions with the Peruvian people, I was amazed and touched by my experiences.

While attending college, I have taken courses to enrich my cultural studies, and I participated in three academic Study Abroad programs. The first was to Australia and New Zealand in the winter of 2012, the next to Japan in the fall of 2012, and the third to Costa Rica in the summer of 2013.

In recent summers, I toured Romania, Hungary, Germany, Austria, the Czech Republic, France, Belgium, the Netherlands, and Luxembourg, which have enriched my cultural experiences and perspective.

Through studies and travels, I have learned about many cultures and had countless adventures abroad. This first edition in the *Savvy Traveler's* series gives you a taste of the sumptuous sites and exciting experiences that await you in Australia, New Zealand, and Fiji.

AUSTRALIA:

Melbourne

Sydney

Cairns

THE SAVVY TRAVELER'S GUIDE TO FUN DOWN UNDER

http://cruises.about.com/od/australiaandnzcruises/ig/South-Pacific-Cruise-Maps/australia-map.htm

Melbourne, Australia

Melbourne is the capital of the state of Victoria, the second largest city in Australia, and is home to the world's most extensive tram system. The metropolitan area is situated in the southwest portion of the continent on the rim of Port Phillip Bay, into which the Yarra River runs, after winding through a great portion of the city. The four million people who live there refer to themselves as "Melburnians." Referred to by locals as the "Garden City," it is a huge cultural center, full of shopping museums, and restaurants, as well as a rich nightlife. There are numerous sites in and around Melbourne worth visiting for everyone.

Need a helping Hand?

For backpackers traveling around Australia, take advantage of the services of The Friendly Group to help you find accommodations and excursions. Visit their website or write them an e-mail at:

www.friendlybackpackertravel.com/traveldesk@friendlygroup.com.au

Want to fit in with the locals?

When you speak the city's name, avoid the phonetic pronunciation of "Mel-born." Instead, try your Aussie accent on for size, and say "Mel-bun"—they'll be impressed by your effort.

Melbourne Visitor's Centre

In this building within Federation Square, visitors can find all the information for their travels and exploration in the Melbourne area. Look for brochures and help with bookings and travel ideas at their help desk.

National Gallery of Victoria

The National Gallery of Victoria (NGV) houses contemporary and historic artwork from a range of artists. The NGV collection is divided into two sites. The first is The Ian Potter Centre: NGV Australia, located at Federation Square. It is the home of the gallery's Australian art, both Indigenous and non-Indigenous, dating from the colonial period to the present day. Works include paintings, photography, prints and drawings, sculpture and decorative arts, and fashion, textiles, and jewelry. The second gallery is the NGV International, at 180 St Kilda Road, which contains the international artwork collections. The majority of the NGV galleries are free to view, and admission fees only apply to some of the temporary exhibitions.

Melbourne Museum

At the Melbourne Museum you can visit the Bunjilaka Aboriginal Cultural Centre to view an extensive exhibit of Aboriginal art and history. There are numerous rotating exhibits, so make sure to check out what is currently showing in addition to the many that are permanent. These include Dinosaur Walk, The Melbourne Story, The Mind: Enter the Labyrinth, Bugs Alive!, Marine Life: Exploring Our Seas, The Human Body, and Darwin to DNA.

Newman College

Historic Newman College first opened in 1918. It is a branch of the University of Melbourne and a co-educational residential college, designed by renowned architect Walter Griffin. The buildings are stunningly beautiful, from the brick outdoor hallways to its pointed spires.

Shrine of Remembrance

With its eternal flame, this special shrine was originally built to honor the men and women from the state of Victoria who served in WWI. It now stands to memorialize all Australians who have served in war. The building houses a visitor center which includes the Hall of Columns, the Gallery of Medals, the Remembrance Garden, an education center, an audio-visual center, a gallery space, a retail shop, and an entry courtyard.

Melbourne Golden Mile Heritage Trail

The Golden Mile Heritage Trail is a fun and unique activity. This walking tour teaches participants how the discovery of gold shaped the city and takes you inside some of the historical buildings along the way. If you choose the guided tour, it departs from the Melbourne Visitor's Centre daily, at 10:00 a.m. and takes approximately two hours to complete. You can also opt to follow the round brass discs in the sidewalk on your own, using the Golden Mile booklet that is available for AUD $8.

St. Kilda Beach

Be sure to spend a day at the most famous sandy spot in Melbourne, St. Kilda Beach on Port Phillip Bay. In addition to sand and surf, you can visit the promenade, the harbor, the pier, the sea baths, marine clubs, and restaurants there. Or if you like to be active, try rollerblading, windsurfing, paddle boarding, swimming, sailing, kite-surfing, boating, skydiving, snorkeling, or jet skiing. There are also plenty of bars and lots of nightlife to enjoy in the area.

State Library of Victoria

The impressive State Library of Victoria opened in 1856 and today houses over two million books. Near the entrance are a pair of bronze lions, as well as statues of Joan of Arc, St. George and the Dragon, and other historical figures. Its expansive front lawn serves as a popular spot to sit and relax or enjoy your lunch. There's no end to the resources inside; take a tour and you'll surely be amazed.

Luna Park

Situated above St. Kilda Beach, Luna Park overlooks Port Phillip Bay. The amusement park celebrated its 100th birthday in 2012 and offers attractions for people of all ages and a wide variety of rides. Its Scenic Railway Roller Coaster is the oldest continually operating wooden coaster in the world.

Looking to explore the nightlife?

There are an abundance of nightclubs and bars to enjoy in the city if you are looking to mingle, dance, or simply enjoy a drink. Don't miss out on my favorite places to party all night: La Di Da, The Lion, Cookie, and Cherry.

Daytrips from Melbourne

Outside the city you'll find breathtaking scenery with gorgeous beaches, wildlife sanctuaries, and numerous excursions to choose from and enjoy. Although it's possible to take the "self tour" option, if you'd prefer to make bookings ahead of time, many tours are available through your hotel, the Melbourne Visitors Centre, or travel agencies in Melbourne.

Great Coast Road

Drive 245 km (152 miles) southwest of Melbourne to experience the Great Coast Road. Along the route, view the spectacular coastline with unusual and breathtaking rock formations like the Twelve Apostles, Gibson Steps, Loch Ard Gorge, Bay of Islands, and London Bridge. There are rivers, rainforests, volcanoes, and wildlife at the Tower Hill State Game Reserve. You'll also travel through a wine region and the town of Geelong where you can learn about the Aboriginal culture.

Phillip Island

Just under two hours from Melbourne, drive or bus to Summerland Beach at the southern tip of the island to view the fairy penguin parade. Be sure to book your viewing ahead of time at the Melbourne Visitors Centre or at your hotel. There are three levels of viewing tickets, and I recommend the "Penguins Plus" where you get to see the tiny creatures up close and personal without paying for the most expensive tour. The little penguins arrive home by the hundreds at dusk, after a day at sea, to rest for the night in the sand dunes. They waddle past in groups, sometimes in single file, for nearly an hour. Unfortunately, photography is not allowed.

WARNING: Cuteness alert!

Maru Koala and Animal Park

"Get in touch with wildlife" at this family friendly park. The enjoyable exhibits feature a variety of Australian animals that you can view, feed, and even pet! There's an eighteen-hole miniature golf course for your entertainment, too. For more information about the park, visit:

http://www.marukoalapark.com.au/

Bendigo

In the gold rush town of Bendigo, just ninety minutes northwest of Melbourne, you can walk all around town to visit the wonderful cultural and historic sites. Go down in an old gold mine, explore the Soldiers Memorial Museum, take the Vintage  Talking Tram tour, and visit the 1860's Chinese Joss House. Walk through the Bendigo Art Gallery, make your own pottery, take a walk in Whipstick Forest, and ride Australia's highest vertical slide at the Discovery Science and Technology Center. Don't miss the beautifully decorated Golden Dragon Museum to see Loong, the world's oldest Imperial Dragon, and the lovely gardens near the entrance.

Mornington Peninsula National Park

Just over an hour south of Melbourne, is Cape Schanck, in Mornington Peninsula National Park. You'll find beaches, tide pools, scenic trails, and beautiful ocean views. Formations like Pulpit Rock and Devils Desk can be seen from a lookout. While exploring the trails, you might catch a glimpse of an echidna in its natural habitat— if you're lucky! There's also a lighthouse, museum, and the former lighthouse keeper's  cottage constructed in 1859. Fees apply to view the lighthouse buildings.

Healesville Sanctuary

At the Healesville Sanctuary, just over an hour east of Melbourne, view Australian wildlife in a natural-style habitat. See wallabies, dingoes, wombats, emus, Tasmanian devils, koalas, echidnas, platypus, and a variety of reptiles. If you're lucky, you can pet the dingoes while they are on their walks. Make sure to stick around for the fascinating "Spirit of the Sky" bird show, and of course, don't leave without petting the kangaroos!

AUSTRALIA

Ibirooroo Balnarring Community Wetlands

At the Balbirooroo Balnarring Wetlands, about forty miles south of Melbourne, there are trails, viewing platforms, and places to observe the local wetland flora and fauna. Watch for a variety of birds, including ducks, swamphens, egrets, cormorants, chestnut teals, and the beautiful black swan.

Bushrangers Bay

This beautiful beach park south of Melbourne features a number of walking trails and a beautiful sandy beach surrounded by breathtaking basalt cliffs. The drive there from the city also offers lovely coastal scenery.

Yarra Ranges National Park

Just over fifty miles east of Melbourne is Mount Donna Buang summit, a local favorite area for picnics, hiking, and biking. The nearly seventy foot high observation tower there offers spectacular views of Melbourne, Mount Baw Baw and the Alps, the Dandenong and Cathedral Ranges, and the Yarra Valley. On the Donna Buang mountainside, you can visit the Rainforest Gallery. At this site, there's a raised observation platform that's fifteen meters (49 ft.) above the ground for viewing the rainforest canopy. Be sure to walk the gorgeous 350 meter (1148 ft.) walkway, which winds down through the rainforest to the gully below.

Sydney, Australia

Sydney is the capital of the state of New South Wales, situated on the coast of the Tasman Sea in southeast Australia. With a population of over four million people, it is Australia's largest city, and the locals call themselves "Sydneysiders." Sydney is renowned for its architecture, parks and open spaces, festivals, and cultural attractions. The metropolis has a wonderful transit system for visiting all the sites, including museums, historical buildings, restaurants, and many nightclubs.

Sydney Opera House

The Sydney Opera House is a world-class performing arts center and a late-modern architecture masterpiece. It is a truly unique building and a beautiful sight to behold. There are always numerous shows playing, so make sure to go inside and look at the schedule for these amazing performances.

Fort Denison

On the tiny island of Pinchgut in Sydney Harbor, stands a former jail site known as Fort Denison, constructed with, and completed in 1857. This historic site was converted into a restaurant, and access is via ferry. Following local tradition, the One O'Clock Gun is fired most days, just as it was from 1906 to 1942 when it was used by sailors to set their chronometers to the local time.

Sydney Harbor Bridge

A local landmark, the Sydney Harbor Bridge is 134 meters (440 feet) at its highest point. Four different climbs are available during the day for a variety of views from dawn to dark. Several million people have climbed to its summit. If you don't want to do the bridge climb, you can walk along the pedestrian path for a brilliant view of the harbor and the Opera House.

Royal Botanic Gardens

Right in the heart of Sydney lies thirty hectares of tranquility and beauty in the Royal Botanic Gardens. Established in 1816, the gardens are at the edge of Sydney Harbor, wrapped around Farm Cove. Take a stroll, relax, and unwind in this bit of paradise inside the city.

Looking to explore the nightlife?

Climb aboard an Oz Party Bus for a fun-filled ride and pub crawl to some of the best nightclubs and bars in the city. There's a light show, music, and dancing onboard with a live DJ and MC, and a professional party host helps with food and beverage deals at all the local venues you visit. Or, head to the incredible three-level 3 Wise Monkeys Pub for food, drinks, and fun! If you're lucky, you'll catch a set of a live band playing on the third floor. Find more information at:

http://www.ozpartyevents.com/

http://www.3wisemonkeys.com.au/

Daytrips from Sydney

A number of interesting and scenic day trips can be can be taken from Sydney. Below are just a few suggestions.

Hunter Valley

Just a two-hour drive north of Sydney is Hunter Valley. This is wine country, and tours are available to visit wineries and the lovely Hunter Gardens.

National Park and Blue Mountains

A two-hour drive west of Sydney, the park is listed with World Heritage, noted for its breathtaking views, including the Three Sister rock formation of Aboriginal legend. Nearby are the historic town of Katoomba and Scenic World, where you can ride the Scenic Railway to the ancient rainforest. Also close by are the Jenolan Caves, filled with limestone formations, and the historic Caves House, a Tudor-style building from the Victorian era listed with World Heritage.

Australian Reptile Park

Less than one hour north of Sydney, this park is home to birds, mammals, reptiles, spiders, and amphibians, mostly from Australia, and some from around the world in the "hands-on zoo." While in the area you can also take a dolphin-watching cruise.

Bondi Beach

Located in a suburb of Sydney, this is one of Australia's most famous beaches. It's nearly one km (over 3000 ft.) long white sandy stretch is patrolled by lifeguards for your swimming enjoyment.

Photo courtesy of: http://www.weekendnotes.com

Manly

A northern suburb of Sydney, the area known as Manly is the home to the Northern Beaches. It is the perfect spot for shopping, dining, walks, views, galleries, museums, and other activities.

Cairns, Australia

Cairns is a city of less than 200,000 people at the north end of Queensland, Australia. It is a seaport, and sugar cane is still grown outside the city. With its tropical climate and proximity to the Great Barrier Reef, Cairns is a popular location for international tourists to enjoy the scenery and water sports. There are also plenty of shopping areas, restaurants, and bars with music and dancing.

Want to fit in with the locals?

When you speak the city's name, avoid the phonetic pronunciation of "Cair-ns." Instead, try your Aussie accent on for size! Say "Cans", and they will surely be impressed.

Fitzroy Island

If you want to explore the Great Barrier Reef, consider taking a Fitzroy Island Sea Kayak Tour. You'll begin with a scenic catamaran ride out to the island. After a short safety briefing, you'll have the afternoon to explore the island in a two-person kayak, snorkel on the reef, or enjoy one of the sandy beaches. A picnic lunch is provided.

Esplanade

This area is defined by its impressive saltwater "lagoon" public pool overlooking the Great Barrier Reef. You will also find food, shopping, and live entertainment in the area. Play in the sand, sunbathe, or sit in the grass under a tree in the beautifully landscaped gardens.

THE SAVVY TRAVELER'S GUIDE TO FUN DOWN UNDER

Looking to explore the nightlife?

There is a rich nightlife culture in Cairns, as it is a popular tourist city. There are many bars with dance floors and music to enjoy. Don't miss the favorite party places there: The Woolshed and Gilligan's.

Daytrips form Cairns

There is much to explore just outside of this lively tourist city. Find your sense of adventure and explore the jungle, zip-line through the trees, or paddle on the rivers. Whatever you choose, it's certain that you'll enjoy both your excursions and the scenery.

AJ Hackett Bungy Jump

Check out the website for more information on the world's only sixteen style bungy jumping menu:

www.ajhackett.com/cairns/activities

Tully River White Water Rafting

This photo was printed with the permission of Raging Thunder Pty Ltd.

Take a white water rafting trip on the Tully River with Raging Thunder, the company who's been doing tours since 1985. Their highly competent guides teach safety measures to you and your rowing team before the trip downriver begins. All equipment is provided, no experience is needed, and the trip includes lunch on the riverside. Just bring your swimsuit (or clothing you don't mind getting wet), towel, secure shoes, sunscreen, and money to purchase the great professional pictures. Find out more about their exciting rafting options here:

http://www.ragingthunder.com.au/

Daintree Rainforest

Visitors can ride a riverboat in to the Daintree Rainforest—just a short drive from the city. Stay at a local lodge or one of several hostels within the forest. Don't forget to book adventures such as zip- lining, horseback riding on the beach, and guided walks to see the rainforest flora and fauna.

Cape Tribulation

Take a drive up the coast to Port Douglas, under two hours from Cairns, and on in to the village of Cape Tribulation, where the Great Barrier Reef meets the Daintree Rainforest. While there you can go kayaking, take a river cruise or a bush walk, or be adventurous and go zip-lining above the rainforest canopy. Enjoy a variety of animal life and an abundance of plant life there too. A variety of accommodations are available.

NEW ZEALAND's

North Island:

Auckland

THE SAVVY TRAVELER'S GUIDE TO FUN DOWN UNDER

http://www.library.utexas.edu/maps/australia/new_zealand_admin_2006.jpg

Auckland, New Zealand

Located on the North Island of New Zealand, on the Hauraki Gulf in the South Pacific Ocean, Auckland is the country's largest metropolitan area. There are almost one and one half million residents, including the largest population of Polynesians in the world. There is plenty to do, including shopping, restaurants, visits to museums and cultural centers, and of course, the nightlife.

Want to fit in with the locals?

Use the expression "Sweet as!" In New Zealand, this phrase has multiple meanings. It can be a substitution for "good" or "cool," as well as an affirmative statement in the place of "yes," "right," or "okay." It is also used as a descriptive phrase, such as, "The waves were sweet as today, mate!"

Sky Tower

Be sure to visit the tallest manmade structure in New Zealand, Auckland's very own Sky Tower. During your ride up to the top, watch the city shrink below you from the glass-front elevator. You can enjoy breathtaking views from the three viewing platforms on this 328 meter (1076 ft.) tower. There are six main areas in the tower. From bottom to top: the gift shop, Sky Lounge Café, the Main Observation Level including areas with glass floors, the spinning restaurant, Orbit, the Sky Jump, and a second and higher level called the Sky Deck.

Auckland Museum

This historic building, surrounded by a beautiful garden, is home to the world's largest Maori and Pacific Island collection. Included in the cultural exhibits and artifacts are an 1870's storehouse, along with weapons, tools, carvings, and animal skeletons. There is also an impressive and beautiful wharenui, or Maori meetinghouse, built in 1878. When you enter this sacred area, be sure to remove your shoes according to custom.

One Tree Hill

This volcanic cone in Auckland houses a tower at the summit where tourists can enjoy breathtaking views of the city. Below its summit, the volcano also has a lava field, three craters, and open fields.

Unitec Mt. Albert Campus

The Unitec Mt. Albert Campus is located ten minutes from the central business district in Auckland, in a fifty-five hectare (0.21 sq. mi.) oasis. Surround by gardens, trees, and lawn, the campus is beautiful and in tune with Auckland's love of nature. Wairaka Stream, which runs through Unitec, is home to many pukeko, or New Zealand swamp hens, as well as several fish species. In addition, there are extensive and lush walking trails to explore in the areas surrounding the university. There you can find many hidden beauties, including a natural waterfall that is a favorite local swimming spot.

Mount Eden

From the top of Mount Eden, an extinct volcano and the highest point in Auckland, you have a 360 degree view of Auckland and its surrounding areas. The fifty meter (164 ft.) deep crater is now grassy pasture for the local cattle to graze in.

Auckland Bridge Bungy Jump

For a true New Zealand adventure, book a bungy jump off the Auckland Bridge with AJ Hackett Bungy. Enjoy incredible views of Waitemata Harbour during the exclusive bridge walk that takes you out to the jump platform. You can even choose an ocean dip during your jump—how refreshing! Get information about this and other fun options here:

http://www.bungy.co.nz/

http://www.gobook.co.nz/auckland/auckland-bridge-climb-bungy-1

Looking to explore the nightlife?

There are many fun places to enjoy the night in the city. Whether you like nightclubs or bars, dancing or meeting new people, don't miss out on the fun. My favorite spots in Auckland were Globe Bar, 1885 Britomart, and Carpark,. You can find more about them here:

http://www.globeauckland.wordpress.com/   http://www.1885.co.nz/

http://www.showcasehospitality.co.nz/microsite/the-carpark

Daytrips from Auckland

Wonderful excursions within a couple hours of the city are available. You can visit the Maori Cultural Center, the glowworm caves, islands with volcanic terrain, and Hobbiton, where the Shire from "The Lord of the Rings" trilogy and "The Hobbit" were filmed.

Waitakere Ranges Regional Park

On the western coastline, just a thirty minute drive from Auckland, lies the expansive Waitakere Ranges Regional Park. This forest is home to numerous waterfalls, rivers, beaches, and giant kauri trees. Make sure to stop in at the Arataki Visitors Centre to find information on the park's wonderful hiking trails.

Waitomo Caves

A spelunker's paradise awaits you, less than a two and a half hour trip south of Auckland. The Waitomo Caves are a series of three main caves systems, full of indigenous glowworms and natural cave formations. Guided tours are available, which include an oral history and explanation of the cave series' fascinating geology. The exploration begins with the Waitomo Glowworm Caves, by boat or inner tube. Next, Ruakuri Cave hosts New Zealand's longest underground guided walking tour. Last but not least, is Aranui Cave, the smallest and most fragile in the system. Inside lives a colony of cave wetas, an insect common to New Zealand, as well as brilliant formations such as stalactites, stalagmites, and flowstones.

Muriwai Beach

Thirty-five minutes due west of Auckland lies this black sand beach. A famous spot for surfing, swimming, and fishing, Muriwai is home to one of New Zealand's only mainland Gannet breeding colonies, the Takapu Refuge. If you visit to enjoy the beautiful volcanic black sand, you may take a stroll along the beach or sunbathe. In addition, don't forget to explore the rock platform that overlooks the beach—but watch out for the giant waves that splash high and without warning!

Tiritiri Matangi Wildlife Sanctuary

New Zealand's Tiritiri Matangi Island, located thirty km (18.6 mi.) northeast of Auckland, is the home to the Tiritiri Matangi Wildlife Sanctuary. From 1984 to 1994, this former farmland was reforested to leave only 40% of the island as grassland. All natural predators were removed to make a new home for threatened and endangered birds and reptiles. Among the species introduced were two extremely rare flightless birds, the takahe and the tuatara, whose ancestors can be traced back to the time of the dinosaurs.

Piha Beach

The most famous surfing beach in New Zealand, Piha Beach is only forty km (25 mi.) west of Auckland. Also referred to as one of the most dangerous beaches, the wild and wind-swept surf of Piha rolls onto the black sand shore from the Tasman Sea.

Hobbiton Movie Set Tours

On rolling farmland just outside the town of Matamata, only two hours southeast of Auckland, lies the setting for the Shire, a piece of J.R.R. Tolkien's Middle-earth. The movie set was originally constructed for the filming of the *Lord of the Rings* trilogy, and has been recently refurbished for *The Hobbit: An Unexpected Journey*. Fans will love the natural setting as they walk through Hobbiton. Visit the party tree, the outside of Bilbo's Hobbit hole, the lake, the bridge, and the Green Dragon Inn—where you can sit inside and enjoy a complimentary drink.

Te Puia New Zealand Maori Arts and Crafts Institute

Visit this incredible center just three hours southeast of Auckland to learn about and enjoy the native culture of New Zealand. This center was established to educate the public and preserve the culture and traditional arts of the Maori people. Don't miss out on the geothermal valley, the Kiwi Conservation Centre, Maori village, or the craftsman at work. Songs and dances of this ancient culture are performed by professionals daily.

FIJI:

Beachcomber Island

THE SAVVY TRAVELER'S GUIDE TO FUN DOWN UNDER

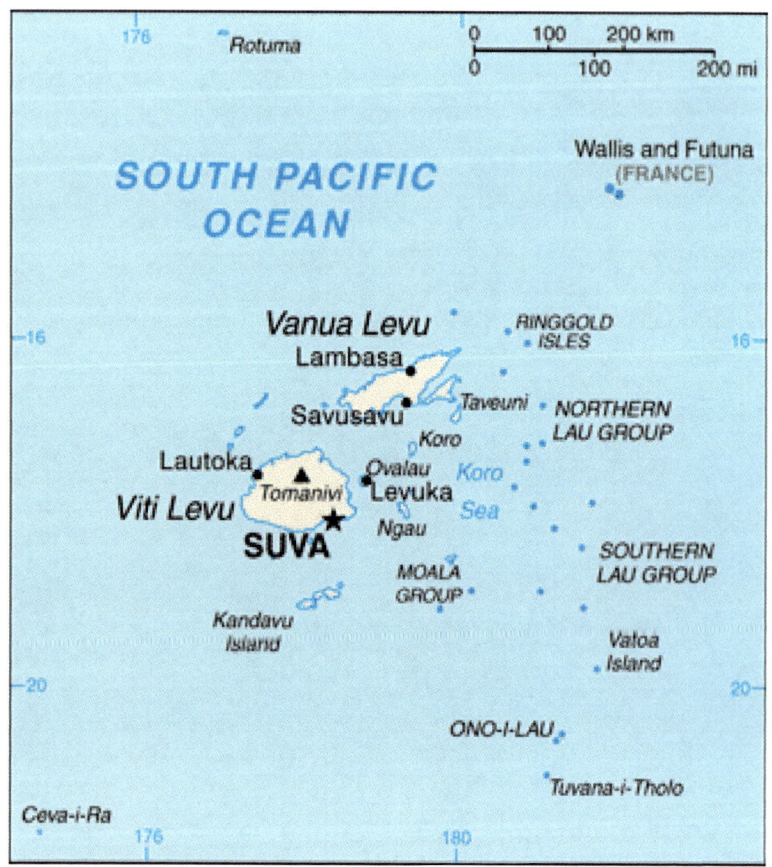

http://en.wikipedia.org/wiki/Vanua_Levu

Beachcomber Island, Fiji

Flights to Fiji from Auckland only take around one and a half hours. The Fijian people welcome you at the airport with warm smiles, and sometimes shell necklaces. Fiji is located 1100 nautical miles to the northeast of New Zealand's North Island. Most of its 333 islands are uninhabited.

Fiji's Beachcomber Island

The Beachcomber Island Resort is a small island encircled with a white, sandy beach, exclusive to resort guests, and managed by the friendly and welcoming staff. Play or relax by day, and party through the night in your choice of living accommodations.

Delicious meals are included, and a variety of water sports and excursions are available for an additional fee. You can swim, get a massage, go snorkeling, go diving, go sailing or parasailing, or just lie on the beach in the sun enjoying the crystal-clear water and sipping on a refreshing cocktail. Beachcomber gives travelers a superb taste of the many astonishing Fijian island paradises and allows guests to experience a taste of the Fijian culture.

Want to fit in with the locals?

When you greet someone new, say "Bula!", pronounced "boo-lah." This word is used to say "welcome," "hello," "goodbye," or "love" in Fijian, although the literal translation is "life." It is an extremely commonly used word, and you will quickly acclimate to hearing it often throughout the day. Also, "vinaka," pronounced "vee-na-ka" means "thank you."

You may be invited to try kava, a traditional drink made with water and the roots of the kava plant, customarily used to relax at the end of the day. It is tan in color and has a strong, pungent taste that leaves a tingling sensation on the tongue.

The Author Down Under:

ABOUT THE AUTHOR

Overlooking Neuschwanstein Castle in Bavaria, Germany.

Caitlyn E. Moore began traveling with her parents as an infant and has already visited five continents. She has also participated in three Study Abroad trips to Australia/New Zealand, Japan, and Costa Rica. Her love of traveling and learning about new cultures inspired her to begin writing the Savvy Traveler's series.

Caitlyn took gymnastics classes beginning at age three, and ended up on the Show Team. She began ballet lessons at age five and danced in the academy's annual shows through her senior year in high school. She enjoys writing, photography, music, and cooking in addition to traveling.

Ms. Moore currently lives in the Seattle, Washington area, and is enrolled in university, where she is finishing her degree in English with an emphasis in Creative Writing, and a minor in Spanish language.

Made in the USA
Lexington, KY
15 December 2013